CONFLICT OF LAWS AND CONTRACT DRAFTING

VOLUME 1, ISSUE 4 OF BRILLOPEDIA

VINI KEWALIYA

ISBN 979-888530571-6

Contents

Preface

"Start writing, no matter what. The water does not flow until the faucet is turned on".

-Louis L'Amour

Hundreds of students and professors are contributing their work to Brain Booster Articles, we are here to provide ample information about Law and Contemporary issues. Our aim is to provide a platform for today's generation to express their views and ideas on law and contemporary law.

Author

CHAPTER ONE

ABSTRACT

In today's time most of the transactions are concluded with international parties or foreign land. Conflict of Law or choice of law is an area of private international law where parties can enter into contract with international parties and can make choices of governing laws. It seems an easy affair but there are lot of intricacies involved in it. Conflict can only be resolved through meticulous drafting of contract or by making clear choices about law. A clear and unambiguous clause of contract makes convenient for court to decide case. Conflict of law or choice of law is a very subjective area where parties are free to decide the law but certain considerations needs to be taken care. Public Policy, question of law and question of fact, choice of substantive law are few matters which needs consideration. This paper analyses the need of clear choices of law as per law of land and need of meticulous drafting of clauses in contract.

KEYWORDS: Conflict of Law, choice of law, question of law, Public Policy and drafting

CHAPTER TWO

CONFLICT OF LAW: AN INTRODUCTION

The terms "choice of law," "conflicts of law," and "conflicts law" describe the legal doctrines that determine which state or country's law applies to the resolution of a legal issue when the parties, transaction, or both have a relationship to more than one jurisdiction and the laws of those jurisdictions conflict with respect to how to resolve the issue. It is undeniable that rules under law of conflicts doesn't defines the tights and liabilities of the parties but they provide a guiding principles to such cases through decided judgements. Conflicts issues can arise in contract, property, tort, and personal status cases (e.g., marriage, adoption, and paternity). Contract conflicts, however, is said to be one of such area which is full of complexities of jurisdictions because of the wide uses of contracts, and it also involves various laws of various states under a single contract. Complicating the analysis is that each state generally has its own unique choice of law statutes and common law precedent, although the Uniform Commercial Code ("UCC") has tended to create some uniformity in this area of the law. Consequently, contract conflicts law can present a challenge for the transactional attorney involved in drafting and negotiating contracts with multi-state or multi-country contacts.

The scope of conflicts law includes not only the choice of applicable law in a given case, but also issues pertaining to judicial jurisdiction, federal-state law conflicts, and enforcement of foreign judgments.

CHAPTER THREE

MAIN CONCERNS IN AN INTERNATIONAL CONTRACT

Drafting the governing law clause
Two fundamental legal issues affecting every contract are:

1. Whether a valid contract will be properly formed when the parties agree to the contract and
2. Whether a remedy will be available and enforceable in the event the counterparty breaches the contract.

Both of these issues are dependent upon the varied laws applicable and they may also vary from jurisdiction to jurisdiction. As a result, when the parties, the transaction, or both have a relationship to two or more jurisdictions--and it is plausible that the law of any of the related jurisdictions could apply to determine the validity or enforcement of the contract, or to resolve a contract issue or provide a remedy for breach-- it is customary and advisable for the parties to agree in advance on the laws likely to be applicable as part of the agreement itself[1]. Although the agreement on options of law available is not always perfect, i.e. not always enforceable, the parties risk having a court make the decision for them if they neglect to make an attempt at selecting the governing law as part of the contract. Thus, choice of law clauses are common and often treated as a matter of routine, even in contracts that do not relate to more than one jurisdiction.

The drafting of a choice of law clause entails two concerns. First, what law should be selected? Second, how should the clause be drafted? In selecting the governing law, the primary concerns are the party's familiarity with the law and ensuring that there is a reasonable chance that the choice will be upheld in any jurisdiction where a suit may be filed. Other considerations may include the convenience of the parties, substantive law advantages, and even the sophistication of the courts in a particular jurisdiction. If the parties agree to select a governing law other than Indian law, Indian counsel may need to retain local counsel in the selected jurisdiction or obtain an opinion on enforceability from opposing counsel to provide comfort that the client has enforceable remedies under the selected law. A secondary, but sometimes critical, concern often taken for granted is how the clause should be drafted.

A.The Form of the Governing Law Clause

The governing law clause in a contract is usually found toward the end of the contract as a miscellaneous provision. This clause contains the following, or similar, language in its simplest form:

This Agreement shall be interpreted, construed, and governed under the laws of the State of [insert state].

The selection of a laws applicable in contract reflects the party's choice. Although it is preferable to be explicit, situations have arisen where a court will conclude that the parties have selected a choice of law even though the choice is not explicit in the agreement or the agreement has expired by its terms.

In **Salazar v. Coastal Corp[2]**., an agreement selecting Texas as the choice of law expired by its terms, and no written renewal was executed. The appellate court held, nonetheless, that the parties intended to apply Texas law because they continued to act as if the agreement were in place. In **Adobe Resources Corp. v. Newmont Oil Co.[3]**, an issue arose as to what law applied to a letter agreement that was silent on laws applicable. The court observed that in case parties to contract intended for Louisiana law to apply because an operating agreement entered into by the parties adopted Louisiana law, and the letter agreement incorporated the operating agreement by reference.

B. Distinction between Interpretation, Construction, and Enforcement of a Contract

The law that is applicable on the contract is concerned with the issues pertaining to validity of contract or with enforceability of the same or a particular issue arising from the contract. The parties may contractually agree about which law should govern the dispute, but only the forum court can make the legal decision of whether that contractual selection is enforceable. When a contract is construed, the forum court is called upon to supply "gap fillers" for terms that the parties might have agreed in initiation, but failed to include in it. A conflicts law issue can also arise in connection with the construction of a contract if multi-state parties or contacts are involved because the construction of a contract can vary depending on the rulesenforceable to the contract. For this reason, it is wise to draft the governing law clause very meticulously and it is important to mention that the contract is both governed and construed by the agreed law.

C.Drafting to Avoid (or Include) the chosen State's Rules

When under Indian courts enforces the choice of, another law of another State as the governing law in a given case, does the Indian court also apply the selected state's choice of law rules to determine whether the courts of that state would apply another state's law under the facts? The "renvoi doctrine" suggests that the Indian forum court should indeed attempt to apply the law of state chosen for law, rules and adjudge the case in same manner as a court in the selected jurisdiction would have resolved it had the lawsuit been filed in that jurisdiction.

E.g. of Drafting:-

This Agreement shall be interpreted, construed, and governed under the laws of the State of [insert state] (other than its law of conflict of laws).

D. Different Issues May Be Adjudged By the Laws of Different States

It is recognized that if more than one issue arising from the same transaction is presented to the court, the parties may agree that the laws of different states apply to resolve those issues. This concept was expressly approved in **Kronovet v. Lipchin[4]**, where the Maryland Supreme Court gave effect to a governing law provision calling for application of Maryland law in the issue of usury and court applied New York law on the other issues of the same contract.

General concepts and considerations applicable to contract conflicts: An analysis

The following general considerations apply whenever a foreign forum court is presented with a potential conflict law analysis.

A. If there is no Conflict of Law, then court will refrain from undertaking analysis of Choice of Law

Analysis of Choice of Law is a task which changes the direction of adjudication, thus if prima facie there is no conflict, courts refrain from dwelling into it. Furthermore, in cases where the application of one of two possible state laws has no interest in the outcome of the proceeding, a conflict is not presented even if the laws differ in substance[5]. When a jurisdiction whose laws might apply to a case has no direct nexus in the application of its laws in that case, a "false conflict" exists. In this situation, the law of the interested state should apply[6].

The problem of intrastate conflicts between Texas civil appeals courts is rarely addressed in published opinions, but there is an interesting discussion of this issue in Justice Duncan's concurring and dissenting opinion in **American National Insurance v. International Business Machine.** Justice Duncan argued that the majority's statement of the law pertaining to remedies available on a breach of contract claim, although correct within Houston's Fourteenth District Court of Appeals, was contrary to how the law had been interpreted by Houston's First District Court of Appeals. He concluded that the law of the First District should have prevailed because the action was originally filed in the First District and subsequently transferred to the Fourteenth District.

B.Only Substantive Rules are considered material for Choice of Law

In a case when a Texas court tried to resolve a conflict relating with rule of choice of law, the issue is resolved under Texas choice of law rules. These rules, whether common law or statutory, are considered part of the substantive laws of the state. The court has resolved it as choice of law issue as a question of law for the court, which is very crucial, but in determining this court has also undertaken a factual investigation[7]. Lower court rulings on choice of law issues are reviewable on appeal de novo[8].

C. Procedural rules of Forum handling that case is applicable irrespective of Substantive Law Choice

When a court selects the law of another state to govern a contract or issue, or the contract contains an enforceable choice of law clause that selects the law of another state, only choice can be made in respect of substantive law and not the procedural law. Procedural law of the forum is followed as per conventional practice.

D. The Laws of another State Must Be Proved

A Forum may, suomoto or at the option of other party, at any time during the proceeding, takecognizance of law of another state[9]. A party requesting such judicial notice is required to furnish sufficient information to enable the court properly to comply with the request. The court's adjudication of foreign law's applicability is a question of law and not a question of fact.

E. Distinction between a making a forum choice and laws applicability choice

A choice of law clause is not the same thing as a choice of forum (or venue) clause, or forum shopping even though they are sometimes grouped together in the same provision of a contract. The choice of rule clause may be enforceable where the choice of forum clause is not. In Gorman v. Life Insurance Co. of North America[10], the Texas Supreme Court stated that a federal preemption provision which affects the choice of forum is a non-waivable jurisdictional issue while a preemption provision which affects only the choice of law is an affirmative defense that may be waived.

H. Public policy of the forum and governing law

It is true that public policy is a very subjective term and unruly horse, however court will not derogate from basic tenets of public policy. To substantiate a court's abstention to enforce a legal right accruing under the law of another state on public policy grounds, the legal right "must appear that it is against good morals or natural justice, or that for some other such reason the enforcement of it would be prejudicial to the general interests of our own citizens[11]."

[1] Party Autonomy (Art. 3,4) Rome I Regulation, 2009

[2]*Salazar v. Coastal Corp.*, 928 S.W.2d 162, 166 (Tex. App.--Houston [14th Dist.] 1996, no writ).

[3]*Adobe Res. Corp. v. Newmont Oil Co.*, 838 S.W.2d 831, 836 (Tex. App.--Houston [14th Dist.] 1992,

writ denied).

[4]415 A.2d 1096 (Md. 1980). This concept is sometimes referred to as "depecage."

[5]*Zermeno v. McDonnell Douglas Corp.*, 246 F. Supp. 2d 646, 664 (S.D. Tex. 2003); Duncan, 665 S.W.2d at 422; *Ford Motor Co. v. Aguiniga*, 9 S.W.3d 252, 260 (Tex. App.--San Antonio 1999, pet. denied).

[6] Duncan, 665 S.W.2d at 422 (involving a false conflict between Texas and New Mexico law); Ford, 9 S.W.3d at 261 (deciding a false conflict existed between Texas and New Mexico law on a tort claim).

[7]*Hughes Wood Prods., Inc. v. Wagner*, 18 S.W.3d 202, 204 (Tex. 2000).

[8] *Minn. Mining & Mfg. Co. v. Nishika Ltd.*, 955 S.W.2d 853, 856 (Tex. 1996); Ford, 9 S.W.3d at 259.

[9]*Kucel v. Heller & Co.*, 813 F.2d 67, 73 (5th Cir. 1987)

[10] 811 S.W.2d 542, 545-46 (Tex. 1991); see also *Whitten v. Vehicle Removal Corp.*, 56 S.W.3d 293, 298 (Tex. App.--Dallas 2001, pet. denied).

[11]*Schein, Inc. v. Stromboe*, 102 S.W. 3d 675, 695-99, 2002

CHAPTER FOUR

CONCLUSION

It is true that meticulous drafting of contract clause might reduce certain hardships for the part and courts. So, there is need of Uniform International Law for International sale of goods. Today's Convention on International Sale of Goods,1980 (Vienna Convention) is a result of long efforts. It has been ratified by more than ninety four countries by 2020. India has not ratified the Vienna Convention but surely this provides a guiding light for the Indian courts to decide cases accordingly. Indian provisions are still governed by Sale of Goods Act, 1930 and India doesn't find two laws in consonance. It is also true that Vienna Convention is not complete in itself as it is provisions of mandatory and directory mature both, however, Sale of Goods Act, 1930 also becomes obsolete in many aspects like where contracts are executed through telephone or other social media platforms.